OH, RATS!

THE STORY OF *rats* AND *people*

A L B E R T   M A R R I N

ILLUSTRATED BY C. B. MORDAN

DUTTON CHILDREN'S BOOKS

DUTTON CHILDREN'S BOOKS

A division of Penguin Young Readers Group

PUBLISHED BY THE PENGUIN GROUP

Penguin Group (USA) Inc., 375 Hudson Street, New York, New York 10014, U.S.A.

Penguin Group (Canada), 90 Eglinton Avenue East, Suite 700, Toronto, Ontario, Canada M4P 2Y3 (a division of Pearson Penguin Canada Inc.)

Penguin Books Ltd, 80 Strand, London WC2R 0RL, England

Penguin Ireland, 25 St Stephen's Green, Dublin 2, Ireland (a division of Penguin Books Ltd)

Penguin Group (Australia), 250 Camberwell Road, Camberwell, Victoria 3124, Australia (a division of Pearson Australia Group Pty Ltd)

Penguin Books India Pvt Ltd, 11 Community Centre, Panchsheel Park, New Delhi - 110 017, India

Penguin Group (NZ), Cnr Airborne and Rosedale Roads, Albany, Auckland 1310, New Zealand (a division of Pearson New Zealand Ltd)

Penguin Books (South Africa) (Pty) Ltd, 24 Sturdee Avenue, Rosebank, Johannesburg 2196, South Africa

Penguin Books Ltd, Registered Offices: 80 Strand, London WC2R 0RL, England

Library of Congress Cataloging-in-Publication Data

Marrin, Albert.

Oh, rats! : the story of rats and people / by Albert Marrin.

p. cm.

Includes bibliographical references and index.

ISBN 0-525-47762-4 (alk. paper)

1. Rats—Juvenile literature. 2. Human-animal relationships—Juvenile literature. I. Title.

QL737.R666M28 2005   599.35'2—dc22   2004024512

Published in the United States by Dutton Children's Books,

a division of Penguin Young Readers Group

345 Hudson Street, New York, New York 10014

www.penguin.com/youngreaders

Book design by Heather Wood

Manufactured in China   First Edition

10 9 8 7 6 5 4 3 2

Contents

The Rat and I 5

Rat Relatives and Ancestors 7

Rats and Their Ratty Ways 10

Rats and People 19

Yummy Rats 24

Pesky Rats 28

Getting Rid of Rats 32

Rats and Disease 37

Rats to the Rescue 42

Bibliography 47

Great rats, small rats, lean rats, brawny rats,
Brown rats, black rats, gray rats, tawny rats.

—ROBERT BROWNING

The Rat and I

Rats, rats, and more rats.
Good rats, bad rats.
Yummy rats, yukky rats.
Pet rats, pesky rats.
Storybook rats, laboratory rats.
Oh, rats!

When I was a boy, my father managed a big construction company. One day, as a special favor, he let me play in a pile of lumber at one of his jobs. It was fun at first. The wood smelled so fresh, so clean, that I began to build a "fort." Then, in a flash, fun turned to fear. While lifting a board, I surprised a rat. It seemed as big as a dog, for, at seven, I was so small. It had huge shiny eyes and twitching whiskers. "Pa!" I screamed. Then, with my heart pounding, I ran faster than I have ever done before or since. As I ran, I "felt" the rat's hot breath on my back, its teeth about to sink into my leg.

My path lay across a block-long stretch of freshly laid cement. Slipping and sliding, I fell again and again. Covered with wet cement from head to toe, I lost my shoes. The cement workers had a fit, but that did not slow me down. When I reached the end of the cement field, I leaped into my father's arms. "A rat is after me," I cried, bursting into tears. Yet the rat was nowhere to be seen.

Pa told me not to be afraid. Rats were always around construction jobs, he said. If you left food lying about, of course they would go for it. Yet they did not attack people unless they felt trapped. "Take it easy, kid," he said in that calm way of his. "Learn about them; you'll feel better."

And I did.

Over the years, I learned that rats and humans have much in common. Rats are mammals, from *mamma*, Latin for "breast." Instead of laying eggs, as reptiles, birds, fish, and insects do, mammal mothers give birth to living young, nursing them with milk from their breasts. Mammals are warm-blooded; that is, they produce body heat from food energy and have hairy bodies. Cats and bats, wolves and whales, bears and buffalo are mammals, too. So are we.

Among the mammals, rats belong to a separate order, or group, called rodents. This name comes from the Latin word *rodere*, "to gnaw." Rodents are gnawing animals. All have an upper and lower pair of incisors, teeth suited for cutting or gnawing, projecting from the front of the mouth. Shaped like chisels, and as sharp, incisors grow throughout the rodent's

lifetime. If their owner did not wear them down by gnawing on hard things, or by rubbing them against each other, its jaws would lock together. This would cause it to starve. If that did not happen first, the lower incisors would curve inward, drilling through the roof of its mouth and into its brain.

Rodents are the largest group of mammals. Of about 4,000 species—types—of mammals living today, about 1,500 are rodents. Mice are the rats' nearest relatives; they look alike, except that mice are much smaller. Other rodents are the chipmunk, beaver, porcupine, guinea pig, gopher, prairie dog, marmot, lemming, woodchuck, hamster, gerbil, muskrat, and squirrel.

Most rodents are small. The harvest mouse, the family lightweight, weighs less than an ounce. The largest living rodent, the South

American capybara, can weigh 110 pounds. A big rat may weigh two pounds and be eighteen inches from the tip of its snout to the end of its tail.

With furry bodies and pointy snouts, rodent-like creatures have been around far longer than humans. The first human ancestors, scientists say, lived about one million years ago. Ancestors of today's rodents appeared toward the end of the Age of Reptiles 65 million years ago. Back then, dinosaurs, or "terrible lizards," ruled the land. Yet they may never have noticed the tiny mammals scurrying under their feet. Even if they had, a giant predator like *Tyran-* *nosaurus rex*—"tyrant king lizard"—could not have sunk its teeth into so small a creature.

Rodent ancestors probably ate plants, insects, and the remains of dinosaur meals. They may even have eaten dinosaur eggs. In any case, the first true rodents appeared about 57 million years ago. We know little about them; since they were tiny, few of their fossilized remains have ever been found. The dinosaurs had died out by then, for reasons that are still unclear. Their passing, however, allowed rodents and other mammals to take over the land.

Life could not have been easy. To survive, every living being must overcome the same challenges. First, it must adjust to a certain environment, be it hot or cold, dry or wet. Second, it must eat. Finally, it must reproduce so that its own kind may go on through the generations.

Rodents have been very successful as survivors. Think of almost any type of environment, and you will find some rodent living there. Arctic lemmings live under the snow. Gerbils thrive in the deserts of Africa. Flying squirrels flourish in the treetops of South American jungles. These squirrels do not really fly, but glide by spreading their toes, which are connected by thin membranes that slow their descent. Yet no rodents have managed to survive better than the rats.

RATS AND CATS / *In ancient Egypt, people consumed large amounts of grain, which was kept in big storehouses. Rats, of course, were drawn to this ready food supply. The rats attracted cats, which were not yet domesticated. The ancient Egyptians realized they had a ready-made solution to their rat problem. So they started leaving food for the cats to induce them to stay around. Their plan worked, and cats became not only highly regarded animals in the society but later were revered.*

Rats and Their Ratty Ways

Everything about the rat makes it a champion at survival. Of all the mammals, only humans have been more successful—at least so far. Just think about what a rat can do. It can:

- *squeeze through a pipe the width of a quarter*
- *scale a brick wall, straight up*
- *fall off a five-story building and land safely on its feet*
- *rear up on its hind legs and box with its front paws*
- *get flushed down a toilet and live*
- *climb up a drainpipe into a toilet bowl*

There are two main types of rats. The Norway rat, or *Rattus norvegicus*, originated in Siberia, a part of eastern Russia. Over the centuries it got other names, based on its appearance and lifestyle: brown rat, gray rat, wharf rat, water rat, sewer rat, alley rat, house rat. Scientists call its smaller cousin *Rattus rattus*. Also known as the black rat, ship rat, and roof rat, its homeland is southern China.

No matter what we call the rat, its body is built for survival. A rat can collapse its skeleton, allowing it to wriggle through a hole as narrow as three-quarters of an inch. An adult rat's jaws are hundreds of times more powerful than a person's. Large muscles allow it to bite down with a force of 7,000 pounds per square inch, about the same force as a crocodile's jaws. Its teeth are stronger than copper and lead.

Gnawing through bone and wood is no problem—for a rat. A sheet of iron a half inch thick or a slab of concrete four inches thick is no problem, either. Rats gnaw through iron cabinets to get at food, and concrete to get various minerals they need to build bones and teeth. Rats have even gnawed through dam walls, starting floods that wash away entire villages. Mostly, rats gnaw to wear down their incisors. Since these grow five inches a year, rats must keep gnawing or die.

Rats have keen senses, also vital aids to survival. Their hearing is excellent, and they can "speak" over distances of forty to fifty feet. They do this by making high-pitched sounds impossible for the human ear to detect. These signals, apparently, alert family members to the presence of food or warn of danger. Elephants make similar sounds that carry for miles. Only the most sensitive electronic devices can detect such sounds.

Rats are nighttime creatures. If you see them running about during the day, it is because food is scarce and they are desperate to find a meal. Although unable to see well in daylight, they have excellent night vision. An adult rat can detect motion thirty feet away in nearly total darkness.

Yet, to find its way, the rat relies less on its eyes than on its hair. Scientists call it a thigmophilic, or touch-loving, animal. Long whiskers on its face and fine hairs in its coat allow it to feel its way around in the dark.

This explains why rats like to stay in contact with walls while searching for food and not cross open spaces. After a few times on the same runway, rats develop "muscle memory," allowing them to take every twist and turn automatically. Even if you

ATOMIC BOMB RATS—ULTIMATE SURVIVORS / *The United States once tested an atomic bomb on the tiny Pacific island of Engebi. The bomb exploded, sending a giant fireball miles into the sky. Thousands of tons of poisonous dust and ash filled the air, then settled back to earth. The poisons were so deadly that scientists dared not return to Engebi for years, and then only in special protective suits. Upon landing, they found deformed plants and animals, the result of radiation. But the rats, safe in their deep burrows, survived man's most frightful weapon. The poisons had not harmed them a bit!*

pulled down the walls, muscle memory would guide them along the familiar runway. Similarly, tying your shoe or always driving a car on the same route develops your muscle memory.

A natural acrobat, the rat has a marvelous sense of balance. It can scurry along telephone wires without missing a step. It uses its tail for balance, in much the same way that a circus tightrope walker uses a wooden pole. Rat experts believe it likes overhead wires because they resemble vines and plant stalks. The tail also helps the rat balance, and sharp claws help it grasp, while climbing straight up a wall.

A rat is not finicky about its food; if necessary, it will eat anything that will not eat it first. This ability to get nourishment from many sources is a great survival advantage, especially when food is scarce. A rat can eat one-tenth of its body weight every day. If that held true for people, the average adult would need about sixteen pounds of food a day. Now imagine eating sixty-four quarter-pounder hamburgers or thirty-two pizzas. You would burst!

Favorite foods are grains such as wheat and rice, fruits, meats, and fish. Birds' eggs are a huge treat for rats. They like them so much that this yen has become a problem worldwide. Not only do rats raid farmers' chicken coops, in the wild they attack nesting birds. So far, rats have wiped out eighteen species of birds and put forty more on the endangered list. In the past, most of

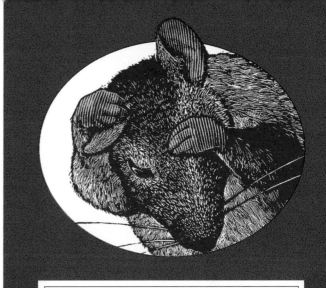

YOU DIRTY RAT! / *Because rats are often found in and around garbage and waste, they are believed to be dirty animals. This is a myth. In reality, rats are fussy about washing and keeping clean. A researcher once watched a sleeping rat wake up, describing its every motion in his notebook: "Eyes open. Rises and stretches. Licks hands; washes face; washes behind ears and continues to lick hands at intervals. Licks fur on back, flanks, abdomen. Licks hind toes, scratches with them . . . Scratches flank and belly. . . . Licks tail while held in hands. Licks hind legs held in hands. . . ."*

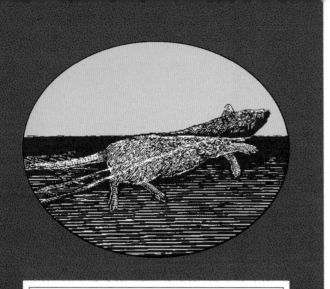

RATS GO FISHING / *Rats "fish" by dangling their tails in the water and wiggling them about. Fish mistake the tails for worms. When a fish bites, the rat leaps into the water and grabs it. Rats will also dive into a stream after fish. They swim in the current and feel for fish with their feet. Rats love water. A rat can paddle half a mile in the ocean, stay underwater for three minutes, and tread water for three days.*

their victims lived on small Pacific islands without native rats. Over the years, however, ships arrived with stowaway rats in their holds. When the ships anchored, the rats swam ashore, ready to meet whatever challenges awaited them.

The ability to survive long journeys and then settle in strange places has helped rats survive through the ages. *Rattus rattus*, the black rat, led the way. About 1,500 years ago, merchants led camel caravans laden with silk and spices westward from China along the "Silk Road." The road ended in the Crimea, a part of Russia bordering the Black Sea. From there, Italian ships took these precious goods to Europe.

We do not know when the first rat scurried aboard a ship. Most likely, it happened about 3,000 years ago, when our distant ancestors first built and sailed ships. Being fast learners, rats found that life was good aboard ship. The dark, damp storage areas belowdecks held everything they needed for a healthy, ratty existence. They drank from the barrels of fresh water kept for the crew. They feasted on sacks of grain and other foods meant for the crew and for sale in distant markets. Ships' cargo, particularly cloth, made for warm, cozy nests.

Oddly enough, despite sailors' hatred of rats, their presence aboard seagoing vessels gave the crews a feeling of security—that everything was "normal." Yet seeing rats swarming on deck, much less rats leaping overboard, was a sure sign of trouble. This made sense, for if a ship sprang a bad leak, the

rats knew about it before the crew, since their hiding places belowdecks filled with water. To avoid being trapped, they scurried topside and then leaped overboard. When sailors saw them do so, they knew their ship was doomed. Then the cry went up: "Lower the lifeboats!" We still say that people fleeing danger in panic are "like rats leaving a sinking ship." Even when a ship was moored at dockside, sailors kept an eye on rats. If they noticed rats leaving their ship, crewmen would refuse to go aboard, because rats sensed trouble even when humans saw nothing to fear.

The brown rat began its travels much later than its cousin. *Rattus norvegicus* made its way overland, across the plains of Russia to Scandinavia, in the early 1700s. From there, it branched out across Western Europe. Within fifty years, it arrived by ship in the New World. The first brown rats reached New York City about 1776, the year of the Declaration of Independence. Today both black and brown rats live wherever people do. Eventually, the Norway rat pushed the black rat out of the cities. Now it lives mostly in rural areas—in the ground, houses, barns, and silos.

One thing is certain: If you see one rat, others are nearby. The reason is that rats are social animals, meaning they live in family groups. Some groups become so large they form colo-

nies of hundreds of members. A tunnel in the ground or a hole in a floorboard or a wall leads to a nest. In cities, the nest is lined with soft materials like gnawed plastic shopping bags and stuffing from dolls. In the countryside, rats line nests with gnawed grass, plant fibers, and wood particles.

Family members enjoy each other's company. They cuddle up together. They crawl over and under each other. Nuzzle each other. Sniff each other. Sleep in warm, cozy jumbles.

In most animal species, the weak and the sick are usually killed or left to die. For example, should a shark get hurt, others, smelling its blood, will eat it instantly. Rats are unusual because family members show "pity" to the unfortunate. Finding a family member with its tail caught in a trap, they may bite through the tail to free its owner. Sometimes able-bodied rats lead blind rats. They do this by allowing the blind rat to hold on to the tail of another or by each holding one end of a stick in its mouth. Families may feed crippled members all their lives.

To survive in a dangerous world, rats must constantly replace those lost to disease, other animals, and people. Thus, female rats have large litters. The arithmetic is awesome. Mama rat carries her litter of six to twenty-two young for three weeks. The young are called pups. After giving birth, she can mate again at once, producing a total of 381 pups a year. Meanwhile, these in turn mate and have their own pups. Laboratory find-

SOLVING PROBLEMS TOGETHER / *An English farmer watched two rats steal an egg from a chicken coop without breaking it. "[I] saw a rat upside down on its back, with a hen's egg in its paws, being dragged by another rat from a laying box across a pigsty and into a rat hole. The erect rat had the tail of the [other] rat over its shoulder. The procession moved forward by halts and starts [as] the leading rat . . . bent forward to drag the other rat along by its tail. . . . So, eventually, the two rats, with the egg undamaged, disappeared into the hole. The distance from the laying box to the hole was about ten feet."*

ings suggest that a single pair of rats could have an astonishing 359 million descendants in three years.

Yet they do not. Diseases and enemies kill many pups. So do rats themselves. Every rat family has its own special scent, another aid in self-defense. Families look after their own, but only their own. Their males defend their territory against outsiders. Should a stranger, whether an adult or a pup, wander into their territory, they will surround it, sniff it, and then eat it. If a nest is disturbed in any way, the mother may also eat her pups. Nobody knows why she does this.

A mother rat nurses her pups for a month. As they grow, they follow her for short distances. They learn by imitating her actions and through their own experiences. Each pup can mate after only two months. It has no time to lose. Unlike a person, a rat is old after nine months. Most die within fifteen months. The oldest rat on record lived in captivity for five years and eight months, equal to over two hundred years for a person.

Rats are highly intelligent and have good memories. Should one eat poisoned bait and die, the rest of its family group will avoid similar bait in the future. Moreover, the first rat

RAT KINGS / *A rat king is not a super-rat that rules the nest, but several rats attached to one another by accident. Rats packed closely in a nest can get their tails tangled. Tails may then become glued together by dried feces and dirt-covered wounds. When their owners try to pull apart, the knot tightens permanently. As many as thirty individuals may form a rat king. Unable to get food on their own, its members would starve without the help of family members.*

to find unfamiliar food may become suspicious and leave it alone. "If a few animals of the pack pass the food without eating any," a researcher notes, "no other pack member will eat any either. If the first rats will not eat poisoned bait, they will sprinkle it with urine or feces."

Apparently, rats can pass food knowledge from generation to generation. Perhaps some chemical in mother's milk teaches pups what she has eaten, alerting them to poisoned bait.

Fast learners, rats can solve problems through trial and error. For example, the sixth-grade students of the Artondale School at Gig Harbor, Washington, wanted to see how their pet rats would do on various tests. They were amazed to find how quickly some learned to get out of mazes. The class's genius, a rat named Squeaks, figured out how to push a ball up a ramp, climb inside a stovepipe, and pull down a tethered balloon to get at a peanut-butter sandwich in a plastic cup.

Classical music, we know, helps develop certain skills, such as mathematics and logic, in the human brain. A controversial study suggested that a rat's brain may be influenced in the same way, helping them learn to get out of mazes faster than other rats.

Rats and People

Humans and rats have never been strangers. Our stored food and garbage have always attracted the furry creatures. Thirty thousand years ago, they lived among the cavemen. We know this because rat bones have been found mingled with those of other animals in caves used by prehistoric hunters. When we first became farmers about 8,000 years ago, rats saw a good thing. They moved into our farmhouses, barns, and silos in search of food.

Despite all our modern technology, rats are still our constant, if not always visible, neighbors. Everywhere, rats invade our homes. They scamper in the spaces between walls and under floorboards. They steal dog food from under the noses of family pets. People returning from vacation have found rats nesting in their kitchen stoves. Sewers and garbage dumps provide a rich diet. Those who study rats say trash-eaters grow larger than their grain-eating country cousins. Farmers report that rats gnaw into the bellies of pigs. If they get hungry enough, rats will even feed on the toenails of sleeping elephants. In Germany, zookeepers had to destroy three elephants crippled by rat attacks on their feet and legs.

People have thought about rats in various ways. Ancient Egyptian texts depict them as burglars stealing into their granaries. In Asian folklore, the rat is often a lucky animal. Japanese people see it as a messenger of the god of wealth. If rats eat the first rice cakes made in the New Year, Japanese believe, a good harvest is sure to follow.

It is the same in Chinese folklore. Chinese believe that people born in the Year of the Rat, which comes every twelve years, have big ambi-

tions and are usually very successful. Unfortunately, Rat people are said to be easily angered and to love gossip.

Most of India's people are Hindus. Because the Hindu religion holds all life sacred, rats are welcome in the temple of the goddess Bhagwati Karniji. To enter the temple, visitors must pass under a marble archway decorated with sculptured rats; more rat sculptures flank the goddess on the temple's silver door. Worshipers donate money to feed the resident rats a mixture of grain, sugar, and milk called *laddu*. During prayers, rats swarm around bowls of *laddu* set on the floor among the worshipers. Calcutta, India's largest city, has Rat Park. There,

rats run around visitors seated on benches or strolling the tree-lined paths. Nobody seems to mind; visitors feed them just as Americans feed squirrels.

People have also used rats for entertainment. "Rat baiting" was once a popular sport in Europe and America. The cruel contest took place in a large room with rows of benches set around a pit. Workers emptied canvas bags filled with rats into the pit. The frightened rats, of course, tried to escape. But since the pit walls were very smooth, they could not get a foothold to climb out. As they milled about, a fierce dog, called a "ratter," was tossed among them.

Trained to kill rats, the dog would bite them,

spattering blood everywhere. Some owners even bred albino rats, because blood showed up better on pure white fur. Meanwhile, the audience bet on how many rats the dog could kill in a given time. In 1853, Jenny Lind, an English bull terrier named for a famous singer, killed five hundred rats in just over an hour. Around the same time, Jocko the Wonder Dog earned the world's record, killing one hundred rats in five minutes. Rat baiting is now illegal in Europe and America.

Today, breeders raise rats for pets, just like dogs and cats. Disease-free and easy to care for, a tame rat usually costs ten to fifty dollars and makes a wonderful pet. Owners can train these intelligent animals to do tricks such as pulling miniature wagons and climbing ropes paw over paw. In schools, rats often join hamsters, guinea pigs, and rabbits as classroom pets. Learning to care for these animals teaches respect for all creatures. More than 550,000 American families own pet rats and mice.

Special organizations bring owners together to share rat lore. In America, the three largest are the Rat and Mouse Club of America, the Rat and Mouse Fanciers for Excellence, and the American Fancy Rat and Mouse Association.

"Fancy" rats and mice are bred for beauty and suitability as pets. The best rats are chosen in yearly "Pageants for Pretty Rats." Judges wearing long white coats with gold-plated rat pins on their lapels select the champions. During a recent contest in Costa Mesa, California, a judge moved from rat to rat. As she

RATTERS IN PANTS / *Some men became ratters, too. These were usually the poorest of the poor, desperate for a few pennies, or the mentally ill. A human ratter went into the pit, where he seized rats in his hands. Then he bit their necks, severing their spines, while onlookers placed bets on how many he could kill within a given time.*

did, she noted things like "Nails need clipping" and "Nice ears."

Fancy rats may also be judged for their personalities. Those raised among people get used to human scent and to being handled. They are often very friendly, as I learned firsthand. One day, a neighbor's daughter put Jean Paul, a white rat with gorgeous eyes, on my shoulder. I was a bit nervous, given my experience with the "killer" rat in the woodpile. But Jean Paul was so gentle, so cuddly, I adored it.

Sometimes rats befriend people. In the 1960s, during the Vietnam War, an American prisoner was held in solitary confinement by the enemy. He was not allowed to see or speak to any other person except the guard. One day, a rat wandered into his cell and sat beside his cot. The prisoner, glad to have "company," fed it from his dish. In time, they became so close that the rat visited him every day. He fed it, played with it, and talked to it for hours. The rat, he said, seemed to understand him. Whether it did or not, it relieved his loneliness. When the rat failed to appear for a few days, he felt sad. When it returned, minus a leg, he welcomed it as a dear friend.

Elsewhere, a bus driver found a young stray rat. It began to follow at his heels like a dog, so he took it home. His children called it Ikey, short for Isaac, their little brother's name. Ikey became a member of the family. As he grew, the bus driver taught him to do tricks. He could sit up on his hind legs, beg for food, and jump through a hoop. At night, he snuggled under the covers at the foot of his master's bed. "Come along, Ikey," the man called in the morning. Ikey jumped into his coat pocket. His master put him in a little space behind his driver's seat, next to his lunch box. Ikey was a marvelous "guard rat." He had such good manners that he never touched a morsel. If anyone tried to take the lunch box, Ikey leaped out and ran up their arm.

Yummy Rats

Throughout history, people have eaten rodents as a delicacy. Roman emperors served their guests roasted dormice dipped in honey or baked and stuffed with pork. On the American frontier, pioneers found possum and squirrel a treat; in some states, people still do. South American Indians ate roasted guinea pig many centuries before Europeans reached the New World; they still do. The World Health Organization (WHO), an agency of the United Nations, reports that seven million guinea pigs are sold as food in Peru each year.

The ancient Chinese called rats "household deer." To them, rats were as tasty as deer flesh, or venison. Rats are still eaten in certain parts of China. While exploring an outdoor market in the city of Shanghai, I saw caged rats for sale. These were not street or sewer rats (described as "filthy" by a dealer who spoke in broken English). Instead, they were specially raised for the market. In certain places, rats cost more than pork or chicken. A pound of rat can be nearly twice the price of a pound of beef.

Restaurants in China claim marvelous powers for rat meat. "If you have white hair and eat rat regularly, it will turn black," said an owner's daughter. "And if you're going bald and you eat rat every day, your hair will stop falling out. A lot of parents around here feed rat to a small child who doesn't have much hair, and the hair grows better."

As in China, rat is a popular dish in certain parts of Mexico. "Boiled in a soup, grilled over an open pit, or mixed in a stew," rats are a delicacy, sweeter than chicken, fans claim. These are not ordinary gutter rats, but grain-eating country rats. Farmers catch them to sell in town markets.

French chefs, famous for their savory dishes,

have various recipes for rat. The famous Larousse cookbook includes one for "Grilled Rat Bordeaux Style." Bordeaux is a famous place. As the headquarters of the French wine trade, this bustling seaport has hundreds of deep stone cellars where wine is stored in wooden barrels until bottled and shipped overseas. Rats live in these cellars, often lapping up spilled wine. If a rat laps up enough wine, it becomes an alcoholic rat. Such rats are supposed to be tastier than ordinary rats. The cook first skins the rat, making sure to remove its stomach and intestines. After that, the cook brushes it with a thick paste of olive oil and crushed shallots, a type of onion. Finally, he grills the rat until tender. "Rat," says an expert chef, "has a slightly musky taste that is not unpleasant." Those who have eaten rat prepared this way compare it to rabbit.

Grilled Rat Bordeaux Style is considered a delicacy. In West Africa, however, rats have become a key part of the diet, almost a necessity of life. Several types of rat, including the cane rat, which lives in sugarcane fields, and the common house mouse, are eaten. According to a report by the United Nations Food and Agricultural Organization, rats and mice make up over 50 percent of the meat eaten in some parts of the country of Ghana. For example, during a two-year period, more than 258,000 pounds of cane-rat meat alone were sold in just one market in the city of Accra. A local cane-rat recipe calls for skinning the animal and splitting it lengthwise. "Fry until brown in a mixture of butter and peanut oil. Cover with water, add tomatoes or tomato puree, hot red peppers, and salt. Simmer until the rat is tender and serve with rice."

Rat meat is rich in protein, and since no creature can live without the right proteins in its diet, some nutritionists believe rats might solve the problem of world hunger. Due to their plentitude, they say rats offer a cheap meat source.

Some U.S. government scientists agree. In a recent research project, they made sausages out of different mixtures of rat meat and pork. Those who sampled the dishes voted that a blend of half and half tasted best.

Eating rat is not very different from eating other rodent meat. The human stomach can digest any type of meat. Thus, it is not the meat, but what we think of it, that counts. If we think something is disgusting and unhealthy, then our brain sends that message to our stomach, causing nausea. A rat raised for food is no more diseased or "gross" than a chicken, pig, or cow raised for the same purpose.

NON-RATTY DISHES / *"People," the saying goes, "can get used to anything." Here is a partial list of foods people have relished over the centuries:*

Chocolate-coated ants

Beetle grubs

Cockroaches

Vulture intestines

Blue jay stomachs

Hummingbird tongues

Mushrooms marinated in urine

Sheep eyes

Earthworms

Flies in honey sauce

Dog, cat, and horse

Other humans—baked, broiled, boiled, fried, raw

Pesky Rats

Most people have nothing good to say about rats. In American and English slang, the word stands for evil. A nasty, dishonest person is called a dirty rat, or just a rat. To rat out someone is to betray them; a ratfink is a squealer. The English call a fool a rat's head. By joining the rat race, Americans begin an endless struggle to get ahead. When you are soaking wet you look like a drowned rat. A person may wear ratty, or shabby, clothes. Such people probably live in a nasty place—a rattrap. When we sense trouble, we smell a rat.

Wild rats are pests. They can't help themselves; it is in their nature. Since they eat the same food humans do, we are constantly at war with them. "Each year," according to one expert, "rats in Asia consume at least 48 million tons of rice—enough to feed a quarter of a billion people. When we talk about rodent control, we're talking about human survival."

In India alone, rats eat or spoil enough grain in a year to fill a freight train 3,000 miles in length. Estimates vary, but worldwide, experts say, rats eat or destroy between one-fifth to one-third of the human food supply. In the United States, the Department of Agriculture estimates that rats spoil over 400,000 tons of food a year with their urine and droppings.

Moreover, rats attack our buildings by gnawing wood, pipes, and walls. Their gnawing of matches and the insulation around electric wires causes fires. Bold burglars, they have stolen keys, coins, and jewelry. Apparently, they like shiny objects. Rats even chew up paper money to make their nests. An Arab oilman distrusted banks. Instead, he stored his spare cash in wooden chests, until rats shredded two million dollars in bills.

Rats also bite people, nearly always at night. While prowling for food, they probably brush up against a sleeping person; when he or she moves, startling them, they bite in self-defense. The U.S. Public Health Service estimates that rats bite some 14,000 Americans every year. According to the United Nations World Health Organization, the yearly number of rat bites worldwide is around a million. Although this may seem like a lot, it is a small number, since three billion people go to bed every night.

If hungry enough, rats may go after people, too. A pack of starving rats once ate a man who wandered into an abandoned coal mine, leaving only his bones. Rats have also attacked sewer workers, but not often. Generally, rats will run the other way if they meet an alert, healthy person.

Rats are most dangerous if backed into a corner. To "fight like a cornered rat" is an expression that means to fight fiercely and desperately. In trying to escape, a rat will leap at its attacker, going for the face and eyes.

If you should see a wild rat, follow my father's advice. Try to appear calm. Chances are, it is more afraid of you than you are of it. Most times, screaming at the top of your voice will scare it away. Running away works, too. As a rule, rats will not follow.

Here is another trick, though you would not want to get close enough to try it. During the Civil War, the Confederate

LIKE IT OR NOT / *It is impossible to keep rats entirely away from farm products. A rat sheds millions of hairs each year. For that reason, the U.S. Department of Agriculture sets standards for the amount of rodent hairs and feces allowed in foods such as peanut butter. Bon appétit!*

prison camp at Andersonville, Georgia, swarmed with rats. When awakened by them, Union captives would take a deep breath and blow on those that scurried over their faces. Rats hate the feeling of wind on their fur, so they flee without stopping to bite anyone.

Avoiding rat attacks is a matter of common sense. Do not look for trouble. If you should see a wild rat, avoid it. Leave nothing for rats to eat. Garbage should be kept in strong metal containers, tightly covered. Do not feed pigeons or squirrels; they can take care of themselves. Feeding them is the same as feeding rats, always eager to feast on chunks of discarded bread. To safeguard children from rat bite, health workers advise parents to wash their youngsters' faces and remove their bottles before putting them to bed.

THE VERY BEST ADVICE / *Rat expert David Alderton says: "The most effective means of controlling rat populations is to make the environment less hospitable to them. Reducing their food supply through improved hygiene is one approach. Today's tendency to leave garbage, including the remains of food, on the streets in plastic bags, rather than in metal or plastic bins, is just one example of how rodents can thrive on human handouts. The high reproductive rate of rats means that they are ideally placed to exploit a favorable shift in environmental conditions."*

Getting Rid of Rats

We have always been at war with rats. It is an ongoing war, perhaps as old as humanity. So far, all our victories have been temporary. For every time science finds a new way to rid us of rats, the rats find a way around it.

Nowadays, exterminators favor warfarin, one of a family of chemicals known as anticoagulants. These chemicals thin the blood, preventing it from clotting. In humans, small doses of anticoagulant help unclog blocked arteries, thus preventing heart attacks and strokes. Larger doses, used against rats, are killers. As a rat eats warfarin-treated bait, or licks warfarin powder off its fur while grooming, the chemical accumulates in its body. Eventually, its blood vessels become thin and rupture, causing it to bleed to death internally. Although rats have a keen sense of smell, they cannot detect tiny amounts of warfarin.

Even so, any anticoagulant eventually loses its effectiveness. This is normal, for although rats may look alike, they are not equal. Certain individuals are naturally resistant to a given poison. Thus, by killing off the most susceptible rats, the poison allows the resistant ones to survive, breed, and pass their resistance to future generations. The result is "super-rats"—rats immune to various types of poisons. This explains why scientists must constantly develop newer, stronger rat poisons. Antibiotic drugs lose their effectiveness for the same reason.

Super-rats reproduce twice as fast as ordinary rats. As the less resistant die, there are fewer rats to share the same amount of food. With more food available, the survivors thrive, gain weight rapidly, and have healthier litters. All poisons, then, have only limited, short-term value. Again, the best way to get rid of rats is to

get rid of their food through proper sanitation.

Over the centuries, we have tried to get rid of rats in countless ways. During the 1600s, Queen Christina of Sweden formally declared war on her country's rats. Her Majesty built a battery of four-inch-long cannons to shoot them with tiny iron balls. Meanwhile, French farmers paraded with torches, threatening to burn rats' whiskers. Across the border, in Germany, townspeople banged pots and pans to drive rats out of their homes. None of these methods worked very well.

The Chinese were more practical. When preparing for winter, they moved out of their homes for a few days in December. A calendar of monthly activities, written about the year 1300, explains why:

> I stop up every hole to smoke out the rats,
> Plugging the windows, closing the doors;
> "Come, wife and children,
> The change of the year is at hand,
> Come and live in this house."

For nearly a thousand years, Europeans treated animal pests as criminals. Real criminals! Until the practice died out in the 1700s, animals faced trial in courts of law. The charges: assault, robbery, damaging property.

This is not as silly as it may sound. Christians based the idea of animal trials on their idea of God. Since God created all creatures, it followed that they shared certain rights. If people were entitled to a fair trial, then so were animals.

Thus, rats faced criminal charges. When they caused trouble, their human "victim" could take out a summons at the town hall. This ordered local rats to appear in court on a certain day and time.

A court clerk read the summons wherever the culprits were seen last. Of course rats cannot understand legal documents. So they failed to appear. The judge then ordered a formal trial.

Rat trials were held the same way as human trials. In the offenders' absence, the judge appointed a lawyer to speak for them. During the 1480s, a French judge ordered a respected lawyer, Bartholomew Chassenée, to defend the rats in the town of Autun.

Chassenée used every trick he knew to prevent the trial. He argued that it was unfair to blame all rats for the crimes of some. When the judge disagreed, he said his clients were too scared to appear. They feared the town cats. The judge then ordered the police to protect the rats on their way to court. When they still failed to appear, he declared them guilty.

Judges sentenced rats to the same punishments as human criminals. Occasionally, they ordered them to leave town—or else. Most rats, however, got no warning. If they were captured, the town executioner hanged, beheaded, or burned them alive. Executions took place in public as a warning to others. Yet the rats, and other animals accused of "crimes," never got the message. They stuck to their "wicked" ways.

Judges had less success than rat catchers. Experts at their trade, these men roamed the European countryside seeking work. Many kings and queens had official rat catchers who lived in their palaces and castles. To identify themselves, old-time rat catchers often wore a pied coat; that is, one with patches of different colors. In addition, they had tall pointed hats and carried poles with large flags. The flags had drawings of rats; often dead rats dangled from the flagpole on strings.

The rat catcher used various tools. When he found a rat hole,

RATS IN COURT / *Occasionally, rats do appear in court, brought by the people they have tormented. Fearing that rats might bite their children, tenants in Harlem, a section of New York City, once protested against their rat-infested apartments. "Bring a rat to court!" the tenants' leader said. So they did. Hundreds of people appeared in court dangling rats, dead and alive, by their tails. Some had rubber rats pinned to the jackets. The bad publicity, backed by a rent strike, called the rat problem to the attention of all New Yorkers.*

he lit a smoky fire at the entrance. As the rats ran out, he knocked them over the head with a club. Often he had a dog or cat to pounce on fleeing rats. Master rat catchers also had ferrets, ferocious weasel-like creatures. With its slender body, a ferret could dive down a rat hole and slash the occupants with its sharp claws. Rat catchers sold their kill for small sums. Tailors bought the soft fur of the black rat to make into coat collars. Artisans made other rat skins into leather for purses, bookbindings, and the fingers of gloves.

The world's most famous rat catcher was German. Legend says that in 1284 rats overran the town of Hamelin. One day, a man calling himself the Pied Piper, because of his costume and his magical flute, appeared. His playing lured the rats to a nearby river, where they jumped in and drowned. When the Pied Piper asked for his pay, the townspeople refused. The Pied Piper began to play again—for the town's children, who followed him to a mountain. Suddenly its side opened and they all went in. Then it closed behind them forever.

Hamelin keeps the legend of the Pied Piper alive. Should you visit it today, you will see in bakery windows pastry rats with candy whiskers. Food shops sell soft drinks in rat-shaped bottles. Gift shops sell masks with rat ears and whiskers. Hamelin's storytellers, however, teach the lesson behind the legend. Honesty is the best policy. Always keep your word—always "pay the Piper."

HAMELIN'S RATS

Rats!
They fought the dogs and killed the cats,
And bit the babies in the cradles,
And ate the cheeses out of the vats,
And licked the soup from the cooks' own ladles,
Split open the kegs of salted sprats,
Made nests inside men's Sunday hats,
And even spoiled the women's chats
By drowning their speaking
With shrieks and squeaking
In fifty different sharps and flats.

— ROBERT BROWNING,
THE PIED PIPER OF HAMELIN:
A CHILD'S STORY

Rats are disease carriers. Scientists nicknamed them "germ elevators," for they bring up microorganisms, or minute life-forms, from streams of sewage that flow beneath the earth's surface. Microscopic bacteria and viruses live in their bodies. Larger creatures such as fleas, lice, ticks, and mites live in their fur. Because of this, rats carry and spread a host of diseases.

An old children's song tells of the worst disease carried by rats.

Ring around the rosy,
Pockets full of posies.
Ashes, ashes,
All fall down.

The song deals with a disease called plague. From 1348 to 1352, it was the scourge of the known world. When plague struck, many people died. One never knew who would sicken and die next. Even staying at home, behind locked doors, could not keep you safe. To calm their fears, children sang while playing funeral.

The song describes the course of the infection. One of plague's earliest signs is a round red rash, "a ring around the rosy." As victims sickened, friends filled their pockets with posies, sweet-smelling flowers to mask the foul odor they gave off. Before dying—falling down—victims often had fits of violent sneezing, a sound children imitated as *ashes, ashes.*

Buboes are another sign of plague. Sick people developed buboes, or swollen glands, in the neck and armpits. Thus, the disease is also called bubonic plague. "Black Death" is yet another name for it. That is because, in its last

stages, victims develop large purple or black spots on their skin.

Whatever we choose to call it, the disease is caused by bacteria called *Yersinia pestis*. This is Latin for "Yersin's plague," named for Dr. Alexandre Yersin, the French scientist who discovered it in 1894, during an epidemic in the Chinese city of Hong Kong. *Yersinia pestis* is a bacillus belonging to a family of bacteria shaped like thin rods. Visible only under a microscope, a single plague bacillus is 1/10,000th of an inch in length. Thousands of them could fit into the period at the end of this sentence. Like all bacteria, it reproduces by dividing into two identical individuals. Each new bacterium then divides again and again. In this way, a single plague germ can become billions inside a victim's body.

At first, *Yersinia pestis* lived in the bodies of wild rodents in China, including rats. A type of flea, the rat flea, lives in rat fur. A giant compared to a plague bacterium, this insect is smaller than a lowercase *o* on this page. Yet it is a mighty creature. Although wingless, it can jump two hundred times higher than its body length. If you could do that, you could easily leap over a sixty-story building.

Fleas feed on mammal blood, which they draw out with a sharp, stiff sucking tube that resembles a mosquito sucker or an injection needle. A single rat can have hundreds of rat fleas. If a rat is carrying the plague bacillus in its blood, fleas will take it in with their sucking tubes. If they bite other mammals, they will pass on the bacillus in turn.

When poisons given off by the bacillus start killing an infected rat, its body temperature drops. This tells the resident fleas to move on. The first sign of a coming outbreak of plague is hundreds of dying rats staggering out of their burrows. If fleas cannot find another rat, they go after other mammals. If people are nearby, they will bite them. Eventually, the bacillus kills the fleas, too.

History's worst outbreak of plague began in China around the year 1333. Called "the Destroying Angel," it killed 13 million people in China and another 25 million in the rest of Asia. After that, it moved westward across the Russian plains in the bodies of fleas and rats that joined the camel caravans.

By 1347, it had reached the Russian port of Kaffa on the Black Sea. A war was going on. To get Kaffa to surrender, the attackers used catapults to hurl dead plague victims over its walls into the city. In other words, they used plague as a "weapon of mass destruction." The tactic worked—only too well. Plague killed most of Kaffa's population, and much of the attacking army besides. It also infected rats aboard Italian ships that had come there to trade for silks and spices.

Before long, infected rats with infected fleas came ashore in Italian seaports. From there, the plague traveled with them in wagons along the roads. It went from town to town, even to distant farming villages, reaching almost every corner of Europe.

Right now, you know more about plague than the most educated person in those days. Nobody knew about bacteria because nobody had ever seen any before the invention of the microscope three centuries later. Ignorant of the cause of plague, or how it spread, people tried anything to save themselves. It never occurred to anyone that rats and the fleas that lived on their fur could be responsible for the sickness.

Doctors who visited the sick wore special costumes. These consisted of a gown that went

from their shoulders to their feet and a hood with a long "beak" to carry spices thought to protect against plague. Yet doctors died as fast as their patients.

By 1351, the plague had run its course. "The Great Dying," as it was called, left about 25 million dead. That is, one in three Europeans. In the centuries that followed, it often returned. Plague died out in Europe around 1732 for reasons scientists still do not completely understand. The last serious outbreak struck Asia in the 1890s, taking 10 million lives.

From time to time, there are still small outbreaks of plague in Asia. In the United States, hospitals treat a few infected individuals each year, mostly those who have been near infected rodents in the wild. Although we must always be vigilant about a serious epidemic, the chances of its happening are slight.

Plague research has taken great strides in the last century. Nowadays, scientists know the disease's cause and how it spreads. That knowledge has enabled them to develop vaccines to make people immune to the disease and antibiotics to treat it. Everywhere, governments and health workers have sought to eliminate rats and the conditions in which they thrive.

Yet this is not the end of the story. Rats are not altogether bad. For despite the trouble they cause, they help us in many ways.

MEDICAL IGNORANCE / *Medical advice was useless, and often dangerous, in fighting plague. Think how you would feel if you took these "simples"—remedies—to avoid or cure plague:*

Gulp a handful of urine first thing in the morning.

Breathe deeply from a latrine.

Sleep with a dead dog under your bed.

Drink powdered gold mixed in wine.

Eat a toad boiled in vinegar.

Chant the magical word ABRACADABRA.

Rats to the Rescue

War is one situation in which rats have proven helpful. The dangers of war continue long after peace treaties are signed and the guns fall silent. Nearly every army uses land mines, buried bombs that explode when a person steps on them, to protect its positions. After the war, these remain deadly, even for generations. The International Campaign to Ban Land Mines estimates that 100 million mines have been laid throughout the world. In certain places, particularly Cambodia in Asia and Mozambique in Africa, they kill or maim scores of innocent people each year.

To permit civilians to go about in safety, land mines must be removed. Experts detect mines with metal detectors or by crawling on their hands and knees, carefully probing with knives. When they find one, they dig it up and disable its fuse. Sometimes a wrong move sets a mine off, killing them instantly.

The African giant pouched rat can detect mines more easily and safely than any human. Up to thirty inches long, this creature stores food in its cheeks, like a hamster. Attached to a leash held by a handler, it lopes across a field and, keeping its sensitive snout to the ground, sniffs for TNT, the explosive used in mines. Weighing just three pounds, the rat is too light to set off mines accidentally. When it locates one, it scratches a few times with its front paws, then pauses. As a reward, the handler gives it a banana, a pat, and some kind words.

Recently, scientists have used the rat's marvelous sense of smell to fight TB, a disease that killed two million people in 2005. In the African country of Tanzania, they have trained rats to detect TB by smelling saliva samples from

suspected victims. Laboratory workers can analyze only twenty saliva samples a day with microscopes. Yet a trained rat can go through 120 to 150 saliva samples in a half hour. The experiments continue. So far, the rats seem as reliable as the human workers. Thus, through early detection, rats may hold the key to saving countless human lives.

Animals such as dogs, cats, monkeys, guinea pigs, mice, and rats are also important in fighting disease. As test animals, each has its special role to play in medical research.

Rats, as we have seen, resemble humans in various ways. According to Dr. Curt Richter of Johns Hopkins University, "The dietary habits of man and rat are almost identical, except that we eat by day and the rat by night. Its short life span aids in studies of growth and aging, and in following inheritance through many generations in a short time. . . . Given the power to create a lab animal . . . I could not possibly improve on the Norway rat."

Everything that can happen in a person's life can also happen in a rat's life, only more quickly. There are rats with diabetes, eye cataracts, high blood pressure, and muscular dystrophy, which causes muscles to waste away. Like aging people, aging rats lose hair, get wrinkled skin, and develop heart disease.

Yet scientists cannot work with just any rat. Each year, in the United States, some three hundred private companies breed over 30 million rats for scientific research.

Rat breeding requires skill. After mating, a mother-to-be is isolated from other rats. When her pups are about to be born, scientists remove them surgically to make sure they are germ-free. Mama never sees her pups. After birth, they are kept in protected buildings.

Nothing is left to chance. Anyone going near a pup must be sprayed with germ-killing chemicals. Air filters keep every germ or bit of dust away from the young rats. They nurse on sterilized milk from rubber nipples and sterilized bottles. Sterile vacuum tubes remove their urine and droppings. No flea ever gets near laboratory rats unless it is part of a scientific experiment.

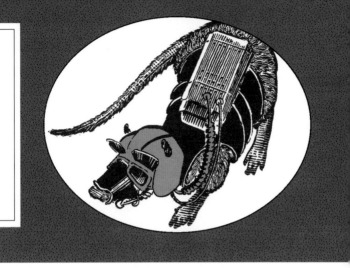

ROBORATS / Time *magazine, in the May 13, 2002 issue, reported that researchers at the State University of New York Downstate Medical Center in Brooklyn attached backpacks with miniature radio transmitters and miniature television cameras to rats' brains. Able to see whatever the rat saw, scientists could then use radio waves to send it in any direction they wish. When the device is perfected, they hope to send rats into collapsed buildings to find survivors.*

Laboratory rats have taught us a lot about how diseases attack the human body. Researchers implant cancer cells in rats' bodies to see how they take root and spread. Government scientists proved that tobacco causes cancer by exposing rats to cigarette smoke. New medicines are regularly tested on rats before being used to treat sick people. For example, the human body has a natural tendency to reject transplanted hearts, eye corneas, and other organs. By first testing antirejection drugs on rats, scientists have saved the lives of countless surgical patients. By law, American children must be vaccinated against such diseases as polio. Dr. Jonas Salk, who developed the polio vaccine, did many experiments on rats to test it.

In the future, scientists hope to use information gained from rats to conquer various human disabilities. Recent experiments suggest that wiring computer chips to rats' brains might enable blind people to see, deaf people to hear, and paralyzed people to move. Similarly, electrical hookups to rats' brains indicate that they dream while asleep. Scientists wonder if learning how rats dream can help humans to learn better and to improve their memory.

Many people feel strongly that animal experiments are cruel and unnecessary, arguing that scientists can get the information they need in other ways. Vivisection—cutting into any living being in an experiment—is a form of torture, say animal-rights activists.

"Vivisection," wrote psychologist Don Barnes in the magazine *The Animals' Agenda*, is "a violation of any basic right accorded to a non-human animal to live unfettered . . . without being subjected to stress, pain, suffering, or death for the hypothetical [supposed] sake of another species or another individual."

Experimenting to save a human life or to prevent blindness is one thing, activists say. All too often, however, animals are sacrificed merely for the sake of profit. There is no need, they argue, to blind countless rats and other laboratory animals to test women's eye makeup. Sensible eating habits, such as avoiding fatty foods, would probably prevent more heart attacks than any number of experiments on rats.

Others disagree, insisting that researchers must experiment either on animals or on human beings. The debate continues. Yet one thing is certain. Without research on rats and other animals, millions of people alive today would have died early or been forced to live with incurable disabilities.

Just think of it. One day, you may owe your life to a rat.

Oh, rats!

Author's Bibliography

Alderton, David. *Rodents of the World.* London: Blandford, 1996.

Burton, Maurice. *Animal Legends.* New York: Coward-McCann, 1957.

Giblin, James Cross. *When Plague Strikes: The Black Death, Smallpox, AIDS.* New York: Harpercollins, 1995.

Gottfried, Robert S. *The Black Death: Natural and Human Disaster in Medieval Europe.* New York: The Free Press, 1983.

Hendrickson, Robert. *More Cunning Than Man: A Social History of Rats and Men.* New York: Stein and Day, 1983.

Hodgson, Barbara, ed. *The Rat: A Perverse Miscellany.* Berkeley, Calif.: Ten Speed Press, 1997.

Marriott, Edward. *Plague: The Story of Science, Rivalry, and the Scourge That Won't Go Away.* New York: Henry Holt and Company, 2002.

Stilley, Frank. *The $100,000 Rat and Other Animal Heroes of Human Health.* New York: G. P. Putnam's Sons, 1975.

Sullivan, Robert. *Rats: Observations on the History and Habitat of the City's Most Unwanted Inhabitants.* New York: Bloomsbury, 2004.

Ziegler, Philip. *The Black Death.* New York: Harper Perennial, 1971.

Zinsser, Hans. *Rats, Lice and History.* Boston: Little, Brown & Co., 1934. Reprint, 1984.

Some More Books to Read

Conniff, Richard. *Rats! The Good, the Bad, and the Ugly.* New York: Crown, 2002.

Legg, Gerald, et al. *Rats (Scary Creatures).* New York: Franklin Watts, 2003.

RAT CARE

Daly, Carol Himsel. *Rats.* Hauppauge, NY: Barron's Educational Series, 2002.

Ducommun, Debbie. *Rats: Complete Care Guide.* Irvine, CA: Bow Tie Press, 2002.

RATS IN LITERATURE

As mentioned on page 36, Robert Browning's *The Pied Piper of Hamelin* is a rhyming retelling of the legend of the famous rat catcher who, when the town reneged on its promise to pay him, led their children away. This is one of the most famous rat tales and is available in many editions. There have been many other books for young readers that feature rats as characters. Some are portrayed positively, even as heroes; some are villains. And in others, the rat characters—like humans—combine both good and bad qualities. You will have to make up your own mind.

CLASSICS

Charlotte's Web by E. B. White (Newbery Honor Book)

Mrs. Frisby and the Rats of NIMH by Robert C. O'Brien (Newbery Medal)

The Wind in the Willows by Kenneth Grahame

MORE BOOKS TO ENJOY

The Amazing Maurice and His Educated Rodents by Terry Pratchett

Gregor the Overlander (and others in the Underland Chronicles) by Suzanne Collins

The Heroic Adventure of Hercules Amsterdam by Melissa Glenn Haber

A Rat's Tale by Tor Seidler

Redwall (and others in the Redwall series) by Brian Jacques

The Tale of Despereaux: Being the Story of a Mouse, a Princess, Some Soup, and a Spool of Thread by Kate DiCamillo (Newbery Medal)